WOMEN'S STORIES *from* HISTORY

Stories of Women During the
INDUSTRIAL REVOLUTION

Changing Roles, Changing Lives

Ben Hubbard

heinemann
raintree

© 2015 Heinemann Raintree
an imprint of Capstone Global Library, LLC
Chicago, Illinois

To contact Capstone Global Library please call 800-747-4992, or visit our web site
www.capstonepub.com

Edited by Penny West
Designed by Philippa Jenkins
Original illustrations © Capstone Global Library Ltd 2015
Illustrated by Jason Juta—Advocate Art
Picture research by Tracy Cummins
Production by Helen McCreath
Originated by Capstone Global Library Ltd
Printed and bound in China by Leo Paper Group

18 17 16 15 14
10 9 8 7 6 5 4 3 2 1

Library of Congress Cataloging-in-Publication Data
Hubbard, Ben.
 Stories of women during the industrial revolution : changing roles, changing lives / Ben
Hubbard.—1 Edition.
    pages cm. —(Women's stories from history)
 Includes bibliographical references and index.
 ISBN 978-1-4846-0863-0 (hb)—ISBN 978-1-4846-0868-5 (pb)—ISBN 978-1-4846-0878-4 (ebook)
1. Women's rights—United States—History. 2. Women—Employment—United States—History.
3. Industrial revolution—United States—History. 4. Nightingale, Florence, 1820-1910. 5. Bagley,
Sarah G. 6. Jones, Mother, 1837-1930. I. Title.
 HQ1236.5.U6H83 2015
 305.420973—dc23   2014015500

This book has been officially leveled by using the F&P Text Level Gradient™ Leveling System.

Acknowledgments
We would like to thank the following for permission to reproduce photographs and artwork:
Alamy: © Pictorial Press Ltd, 96; Bridgeman Art Library: Look and Learn, 4; Capstone: Advocate
Art/Jason Juta, 6, 13, 20, 32, 40, 50, 56, 61, 73, 76, 88, 91; Library of Congress: Cover.

Every effort has been made to contact copyright holders of material reproduced in this book. Any
omissions will be rectified in subsequent printings if notice is given to the publisher.

Contents

Introduction

In the early 18th century in the United States and United Kingdom, most people lived in the countryside, where they worked as farmers or made goods using simple machines.

But from the mid-18th century, new machines powered by steam and coal began to produce goods on a massive scale. This was known as the Industrial Revolution.

People were hired to operate the machines in large factories, while others mined for coal. These people were badly paid and dealt with harsh working conditions. Life was particularly hard for working women, who received lower wages and fewer rights than men.

Some women, however, would not stand for the poor treatment of themselves or others. They dedicated their lives to helping those in need and supporting the rights of workers. Four such women were Elizabeth Fry, Florence Nightingale, Sarah G. Bagley, and Mother Jones.

Elizabeth Fry:
Angel of the Prisons

Elizabeth Fry was a prison reformer who devoted herself to helping the female inmates of English jails.

She was born during the Industrial Revolution, a period rife with poverty and crime. The prison system was very harsh at this time. People were jailed or sentenced to death for minor crimes such as stealing or forgery. But despite these extreme sentences, many people thought prisoners should be locked away and forgotten. English prisons were overcrowded, filthy places that were full of disease and misery.

While many prisoners lost hope, Elizabeth Fry was determined to make their lives more bearable. Known as the Angel of the Prisons, Elizabeth believed that prisoners should be treated with compassion and kindness. Through her reforming work, Elizabeth changed the public view of prisons and improved conditions for those locked inside them.

Elizabeth Gurney was born into a wealthy Quaker family in the English city of Norwich on May 21, 1780. Nicknamed Betsy, Elizabeth lived a life of luxury with her 11 siblings. Her family owned a large mansion called Earlham Hall, where they often held dinners, concerts, and balls for friends. Elizabeth wore fine clothes, ate the best foods, and had enormous private grounds to enjoy.

However, she was a nervous and sickly child. Elizabeth was scared of the dark and could not sleep without a candle by her bed. The sea terrified her and she had nightmares about drowning. Even a glance from a stranger could make Elizabeth burst into tears. But despite her nervousness and health issues, Elizabeth was a kind, honest, and considerate person. She went out of her way to help those less fortunate than herself.

In 18th- and 19th-century England, most people were less fortunate than the Gurney family. The Industrial Revolution had made some people very wealthy and many people very poor. Whole families often left the countryside to find work in city factories. Here, workers toiled for up to 14 hours a day in dangerous conditions for little pay.

As a result of the high level of poverty in the cities, many people turned to crime. The rising cost of bread in the late 18th century caused riots in many cities, including Norwich. But Elizabeth was kept away from these troubles in Earlham Hall.

However, Elizabeth would be unable to ignore the plight of the poor on a visit to London in 1789. Riding through the streets in her father's luxurious carriage, Elizabeth was shocked by the city's slums. While Elizabeth's time in London included opera visits and society dinners, she couldn't help wondering about those suffering in the slums. She felt she could do more with her life than just socializing.

Then, one day, Elizabeth went to hear a speech by an American Quaker named

William Savery. The talk had a profound effect on Elizabeth. She decided to devote herself to helping others. Elizabeth wrote a statement in her journal about how she would live her life from that point on:

First. Never lose any time.
Second. Never err the least in truth.
Third. Never say an ill thing of a person.
Fourth. Never be irritable or unkind
    to anybody.
Fifth. Never indulge myself in luxuries that
    are not necessary.
Sixth. Do all things with consideration.

When Elizabeth returned to Earlham Hall, she began helping the poorer children in the area. She often bought them new clothes and organized classes for them in one of the mansion's unused rooms. There was no public education system in the 18th century, and many children could not read or write. Boys of wealthy families often attended private schools, but it was unusual for girls to be educated. However, Elizabeth and her siblings had been taught by private tutors.

Schools for poor children were not established until 1811. Instead of school, poor children often worked alongside their parents in factories or coal mines, sometimes becoming chimney sweeps. The number of children Elizabeth educated in her makeshift classroom rose every year. By 1800, there were 86 of them, called Betsy's imps by her family.

In the 19th century, daughters from wealthy families were expected to marry. So, in 1800, Elizabeth married a banker named Joseph Fry and moved to London to begin a new life.

Beyond the problem of poverty, London was a rough place during the time of the Industrial Revolution. There were public hangings and floggings, and the city's slums were dirty and dangerous. Although she lived in a large mansion with many servants, Elizabeth often visited the slums to help the poor. She handed out food and clothes and even sent her own doctor to tend to the sick.

Elizabeth would give birth to 12 children of her own, but she always found time to help those in need. She rose at 4 a.m. to fit in all her day's activities, which would soon include the work that made her famous. This began in 1813, when her friend Stephen Grellet told her about the terrible conditions he had witnessed in London's Newgate Prison.

Stephen was a French aristocrat who was trying to reform England's jails. At that time, all prisoners were locked up together, regardless of whether they were murderers sentenced to death or accused people awaiting trial. Inside the prisons, hundreds of inmates were crammed into tiny cells. There was usually no bedding or heating and often just a bucket for a toilet. When new prisoners arrived, the guards demanded a garnish from them. This meant handing over money or, if the prisoner had none, clothes to the guards. Prisons were privately run in those days, and demanding a garnish was how the guards made money. For those without money, life in prison could be very hard. These inmates were often fed only with soup made from water and a piece of bread. Many soon became sick from hunger, cold, or disease.

Newgate Prison had a particularly gruesome reputation. Here, condemned prisoners were executed by hanging in front of a crowd. Before the executions, people could pay to watch prisoners sitting in their cells next to their own coffins. Sometimes the condemned prisoner was a woman.

Stephen Grellet told Elizabeth he had been shocked by conditions for female inmates inside Newgate Prison. Many of the women were sick or starving, and all were cruelly treated by the male guards. Worse still was the sight of many newborn babies, most of whom were cold and naked. When Elizabeth heard Stephen's story, she immediately decided to try to help the prisoners. Armed with blankets and clothes and accompanied by her friend, Anna Buxton, Elizabeth made her way to Newgate Prison.

When Elizabeth and Anna reached Newgate Prison, the warden warned them not to enter the women's cells or they would be beaten and robbed for their clothes by the inmates. When Elizabeth insisted they be let in, the warden unlocked the gates for them. He stayed outside himself, for fear of being attacked.

Inside, the scene was a horror to behold. Here, 300 women were crammed into two rooms built to fit 60 inmates. Some of the women had been sentenced to death and others were awaiting trial. All of the women, however, were in a similar state. They were filthy, cold, dressed in rags, and hungry. Some screamed and shouted, while others lay sick on the bare floor covered only by dirty straw. In the corners, tiny children sat and watched the miserable scene.

The warden had expected the female inmates to attack Elizabeth and Anna when they entered, but instead the prisoners fell silent. Most had been left to rot in jail, with their health and safety ignored by the warden and guards. Being attended to by two well-dressed women was a new experience.

Elizabeth and Anna moved quickly from prisoner to prisoner. They gave out warm clothing, dressed the children, tended to the sick, and ordered fresh straw for bedding from the guards.

Over the next few weeks, the women made several similar visits to Newgate Prison. Elizabeth wrote a letter about her experiences to her sons, who were staying at Earlham Hall.

> I have been twice to Newgate Prison to see the poor prisoners who had little infants without clothing. If you saw how small a piece of bread they had every day you would be sorry, for they had nothing else to eat.

In 1817, Elizabeth returned to Newgate Prison to focus on helping the children there. To do this, she formed a committee called the Society for the Reformation of Prison

Discipline. There were several powerful and influential people on the committee. Because of this, Elizabeth was able to obtain permission to visit the prison any time she liked.

One of the committee members was Thomas Fowell Buxton. Thomas was a campaigner for the abolition of slavery and the brother of Anna, Elizabeth's friend. When he visited Newgate Prison, Thomas was distressed to see "forty-four little wretches, some of them under sentence of death." The death penalty was the reality for many children in prison. Others as young as seven were locked up in iron chains. Some of the youngsters at Newgate Prison simply had the misfortune of being born in jail. These children were at risk of growing up illiterate and learning their behavior from the inmates around them.

Elizabeth put the question to the women of the prison, "Is there not something we can do for these innocent little children? Are they to learn to become thieves or worse?"

With the permission of the Sheriffs of London and the prison governor, the female inmates agreed to help Elizabeth set up a classroom at Newgate Prison.

One of the inmates acted as the principal, while Elizabeth and two friends taught basic education to 25 of the prison children. One of Elizabeth's friends, Mary Sanderson, described entering the classroom as "going into a den of wild beasts." But the class was such a success that many of the women inmates also wanted to be taught there.

With the Newgate Prison classroom up and running, Elizabeth turned her attention to the women inmates. Elizabeth thought that letting the women work would help them regain some dignity and self-respect. She asked the women if they would like to learn to knit and sew. They would have to agree to start work at nine in the morning and not swear, gamble, fight, or beg. The inmates would appoint one of the prisoners as monitor to make sure the rules were not broken. Elizabeth and other volunteers would teach the sewing and knitting. The inmates liked Elizabeth's idea. Now all she had to do was convince the London Sheriffs and the prison governor.

Elizabeth invited the London Sheriffs and Newgate's prison governor to dinner to explain her idea for putting the female inmates to work. The governor and Sheriffs did not believe the program would work, but they gave Elizabeth permission to try.

One month later, they visited Newgate Prison and were amazed by the results. The wild women of the prison had been replaced by workers dressed in blue aprons who sat calmly knitting and sewing. Elizabeth's work program was such a success that it was extended to other prisons in England. In 1818, the English government even asked Elizabeth to discuss her work program in front of a government committee.

Elizabeth explained to the committee that the female inmates had been taught to sew quilts made of scraps of material bought cheaply from textile factories. The quilts were then sold in English colonies such as Australia. The inmates also knit stockings for sale and were allowed to put some of the profits toward tea, sugar, and clothes. Often, Elizabeth told the committee, female prisoners in Newgate Prison had barely enough clothing to cover themselves. Usually these clothes had been taken by the guards under the garnish system.

Elizabeth explained that reforms were needed to make prisons more humane places for women. She said they should be allowed to work, have their own cells to sleep in, and be tended to by female guards only.

The committee was impressed by Elizabeth. In its report to the government, the committee said:

> [Elizabeth's efforts] in the female part of the prison, have indeed, by the establishment of a school, by providing work and encouraging industrious habits, produced the most gratifying change.

In 1818, Elizabeth became concerned about the plight of female convicts. These convicts were bound for Australia aboard one of many transportation ships. Transportation was seen as a way to punish crimes without sentencing people to death. But this meant a person found guilty of stealing could be sentenced to a life of hard labor in Australia.

Between 1787 and 1868, over 160,000 convicts were transported to Botany Bay, in Australia, including thousands of inmates from Newgate Prison. Many of the female inmates rioted the night before being taken to the ships. To get to the docks, the women were chained together in open wagons, which people pelted with rotten fruits and vegetables. It then took up to four months to make the journey from the United Kingdom to Australia. Many convicts died along the way from disease, starvation, and exposure.

To improve conditions for the convicts, Elizabeth convinced the governor of Newgate Prison to transport the inmates in closed carriages instead of open wagons. To help calm them the night before their ship sailed, Elizabeth read to the inmates from the Bible.

The next day, she would see them off from the docks and give every female inmate a small bundle for the journey. Each bundle contained an apron, needles, thread, scissors, and other materials for sewing and knitting. Like her reforms at Newgate Prison, Elizabeth believed that allowing the women to work would make life aboard the ships more bearable.

Elizabeth continued her work with female convicts for over 20 years, visiting more than 100 ships during this time. The sentence of transportation was officially abolished in 1853, although convicts continued to be sent to Australia for another 15 years.

During the 1820s, Elizabeth became a popular figure among the English public, the government, and the British queen. Queen Victoria met Elizabeth several times and donated money toward her charitable work. Elizabeth extended her prison work by visiting the jails of northern England and Scotland with her brother Joseph. Their findings reported many dungeon-like prisons furnished only with dirty straw and a tub for a toilet.

Elizabeth's prison work brought about a change in English law. The 1823 Gaols Act put female guards in charge of female inmates, prohibited the use of iron restraints, and paid prison guards a salary, in order to end the garnish system. Later, in 1858, the interior of Newgate Prison was rebuilt with individual cells for the inmates. This had been another one of Elizabeth's recommendations.

But Elizabeth did not stop at prisons. She helped improve conditions for people in mental asylums and established shelters for homeless people.

In 1840, Elizabeth started a training school for nurses at Guy's Hospital in London. Another reformer, Florence Nightingale, was greatly impressed with Fry's school and the level of training given to the nurses there. Although Florence and Elizabeth were alive at the same time, they never met in person.

For a woman of her time, Elizabeth Fry led an extraordinary life. She had married and raised children, as was expected, but also dedicated herself to helping the lives of strangers. By the end of her life, Elizabeth was so famous that she was inspecting prisons across Europe. She then visited the royal courts of countries such as Prussia and Denmark to give recommendations for improving their prisons. Her advice was always the same. She believed prisoners should be kept employed, given separate cells to sleep in, and for female prisoners to be watched by female guards. She did not believe in prisoners being chained up, treated cruelly, or having to sell their clothes to survive.

Through her principles for prison reform, Elizabeth not only improved conditions for the inmates, but she also made the public aware of the horrors of prison life. This allowed people to feel compassion for those behind bars. It also paved the way for a more humane prison system in England and other countries around the world. Elizabeth is remembered for her groundbreaking work in prisons, but it is her kindness and compassion toward people otherwise forgotten by society that makes up her legacy.

> The good principle in the hearts of many abandoned persons may be compared to the few remaining sparks of a nearly extinguished fire. By means of the utmost care and attention united with the most gentle treatment, these may yet be fanned into a flame, but under the operation of a rough or violent hand, they will presently disappear and be lost for ever.
>
> —Elizabeth Fry

Florence Nightingale:
Founder of Modern Nursing

Florence Nightingale was a famous British war heroine who laid the foundations for modern nursing. Florence is best remembered for helping the sick and poor and tending to wounded soldiers in the Crimean War (1835–1836). However, she was an extremely unusual woman for her time.

Born into a wealthy family, Florence was expected to marry, have children, and never work. But this was not enough for her. Instead, she did the unthinkable by staying unwed and becoming a nurse. By doing so, she paved the way for professional nurses and changed attitudes toward roles for women in society.

Born on May 12, 1820, Florence Nightingale showed an early childhood interest in treating the sick, injured, and unwell. She would often closely observe the illnesses of family members, writing down their symptoms and the care prescribed by the doctor. She tended to a cousin's wrist after it had been injured during a game and treated a farm dog's broken leg by binding it and nursing the animal back to health. Florence would later write in her diary:

> The first idea I can recollect when I was a child was a desire to nurse the sick.

Florence's family was wealthy enough to own two large country mansions in England, called Embley Park and Lea Hurst. Florence and her family split their time between the two mansions. They also spent a great deal of time entertaining, socializing, and traveling to London and throughout Europe. Florence and her two sisters were educated by a nanny and their father, who did not have to work. But while a life of comfort suited her sister Parthenope, Florence felt bored and unsatisfied.

Many children in England were not as lucky as Florence. In the cities, children worked in factories and lived in slum housing with their families. A lack of sanitation in these slums caused the spread of fatal diseases such as cholera. In coal-mining towns, poor diets and damp conditions led to illnesses such as rickets and influenza.

In the early 1840s, poverty also struck the villages around Lea Hurst. Bad harvests led to lower wages for workers, and many were struggling to eat. Florence and her mother helped the poor around them by tending to the sick and often paying for a doctor to visit.

In her diary, Florence wished there was more she could do to aid "the sufferings of man." She wrote:

> All that poets sing of the glories of this world are untrue. All the people I see are eaten up with care or poverty or disease.

Florence grew into a bright, beautiful young women, and her family expected her to marry and have children. In 1846, the poet and journalist Richard Monckton Milnes asked for Florence to marry him. But Florence told Richard she was not ready for marriage and asked him to wait. It would take several years for Florence to give a final answer of no.

What Florence really wanted to do was train as a nurse. But this news shocked her family. "It was as if I had wanted to be a kitchen maid," Florence wrote of her parents' reaction. But for Florence's family, there was little difference between working as a nurse or a servant.

In the 19th century, nurses often had a reputation for being lazy alcoholics. In reality, many nurses were extremely hardworking and dedicated. But unlike today, nurses were not medically trained, and women did not need any experience to work as one. Most nurses' duties consisted of bed-making, cleaning, and serving meals. Only head nurses actually cared for the patients, and their medical knowledge was based on what they had picked up from the male doctors. For many upper-class people, such as Florence's parents, a nurse was little more than a maid who fluffed up a patient's pillows. Their answer to Florence's request to train as a nurse was therefore a resounding "no"!

After Florence's nursing plans were rejected by her parents, she fell into a depression. All she could do with her spare time was secretly read about hospitals and health care. To cheer her up, Florence's parents sent her on a trip to Europe with some family friends. However, the trip did not make Florence forget her dreams. Instead, it strengthened her resolve to make her dreams come true. In Rome, she met Sidney Herbert, an English aristocrat who encouraged her to become a nurse.

Then, in 1850, Florence sealed her fate when she visited the Kaiserswerth Institute in Germany. The institute trained upper-class women to be nurses and had been created by Pastor Theodor Fliedner. The pastor had been inspired to open the institute after seeing Elizabeth Fry's prison reform work in London. Elizabeth Fry, in turn, visited Kaiserswerth Institute, which she used as a model for her nursing school at Guy's Hospital in London. A few days at the institute was all Florence needed to return to England and declare she was going back to train as a nurse. Her parents had no choice but to agree.

In 1851, Florence spent three months at Kaiserswerth Institute learning her trade. She was taught how to dress wounds, give medicine, assist in operations, and apply leeches. She was even allowed to assist with the amputation of limbs, something she found extremely interesting. It was these methods that Florence applied in London, when she took her first ever job, at age 33.

Florence's new position was as Superintendent of the Institution for the Care of Sick Gentlewomen in London. The institution was designed as a hospital for middle-class women without the money to pay for private care. Florence's main job was to ensure the institution was running smoothly, but she quickly began making changes.

She found a new building to house the institution and then turned it into an efficient, modern hospital. To do this, Florence had rooms built to house 27 patients. Pipes were fitted to bring hot water to every floor, which was unusual for the time. She also set up a system of bells, so the nurses could see which patient was calling for assistance.

Some of Florence's patients had serious health problems such as cancer. Others pretended to be sick so they could stay at the institution. One of the patients had been bedridden for three years and believed the only things she could swallow were port wine and cream. After spending two months at the institution, the same patient was eating solid food and walking again.

Florence herself made sure she was present for many of the operations, where she gave anesthetic or sewed up wounds. But the institution soon stopped being a challenge for Florence, who had higher ambitions. What she really wanted to do was train nurses. Florence found most nurses knew little about basic hygiene and tending to the sick and were often undisciplined. Good nurses were in short supply everywhere. In 1854, shocking reports were coming back from the Crimean War about terrible conditions at the military hospitals there. Florence's next challenge had arrived.

The Crimean War was fought between Russia and Turkey, mostly over control of the Black Sea, which lay between the two countries. The British and French had both sent ships and troops to help the Turkish. Most of them arrived in the Black Sea ports of Scutari and Varna. But these places were not equipped to deal with the 60,000 soldiers soon encamped there. It did not take long for unsanitary conditions and disease to strike down many of the soldiers.

Hundreds of British soldiers were reported to have died from cholera, dysentery, and diarrhea before they fired a single shot. Worse still, wounded soldiers coming back from the fighting had to suffer from unsanitary conditions in the hospitals as well.

An article about events at the Scutari military hospital was reported in *The Times* newspaper:

> Not only are there not sufficient surgeons...
> not only are there no dressers and nurses...
> but what will be said when it is known that
> there is not even linen to make bandages for
> the wounded?

When Florence read *The Times* article, her first reaction was to grab two nurses and set sail for the Black Sea. Her old friend Sidney Herbert, then the Secretary of State for War, was thinking the same thing. But instead of two nurses, Sidney wanted Florence to lead a team of nurses to fix things at the Scutari Military Hospital. So, in October 1854, Florence led 38 nurses to the Crimean War. She also had a new title—Superintendent of the Female Nursing Establishment in the English General Military Hospitals in Turkey.

Nothing would prepare Florence and her nurses for the horror they found at Scutari. Over 4 miles (6 kilometers) of hospital hallways were filled with sick and wounded soldiers, who lay on the floor or on old burlap sacks. The hospital was rife with rats, lice, and disease. Most of the wounded soldiers had simply been dumped on the floor and left to hope that a doctor would visit them at some point. Many were left unattended and died from their wounds, cholera, or dysentery.

Florence had been sent to improve conditions at Scutari, but some of the workers were hostile toward her. At first, Florence's nurses were only allowed to enter the wards and help soldiers if they were asked to.

In the meantime, Florence put them to work making bandages from rags, scrubbing the walls and floor, and washing the bed linens. She then organized the patients into a system of numbered beds set out on either side of the hallway, so people had space to walk through them. The management skills Florence had learned at the Institution for the Care of Sick Gentlewomen were serving her well. But she was still unable to tend to the patients themselves.

One month later, hundreds of freshly wounded soldiers were sent to Scutari. Finally, Florence and her nurses were called upon to care for the patients.

First of all, they went through the hospital giving out new shirts to replace those soaked with blood. Next, the nurses bound the men's wounds and made sure they were comfortable. Florence also introduced a screen to be placed around the bed of a soldier who was having a limb amputated. This, Florence said, helped those in the beds next to him not to lose hope.

However, despite Florence's efforts, dozens of men were dying in the hospital each day from dysentery alone. The hospital was later found to have such clogged sewers that human waste was seeping up through the ground and around the building. The rotting carcass of a horse was blocking a pipe that brought fresh water to the hospital. This had contaminated the water. While Florence and her nurses made life at Scutari much more bearable for its patients, they did not deal with the sanitation issues that led to such a rapid spread of disease. It was only after these issues had been dealt with that conditions improved and the death rate fell.

Despite this, Florence worked tirelessly during this period, eating her meals as she wrote reports and requests for supplies. The hospital had a lack of basic supplies such as bandages, mops, and towels. Scissors were also urgently needed for the patients' hair, which Florence often found full of lice.

When supplies were not forthcoming, Florence visited nearby Turkish markets. There, she had the freedom to find the items herself. She bought fresh local food and then set about designing a healthy hospital menu for her patients.

Writing to Sidney Herbert, Florence described her role at the hospital as "cook, house-keeper, scavenger, washerwoman, general dealer and store keeper."

Another problem facing Florence was the quality of the nurses she had brought with her. Some had already left because they did not like the food. Others, Florence had sent home because of drunkenness. Although the nurses' duties revolved around washing, sewing, and cooking, Florence estimated that only around 16 of her 38 nurses could do this simple work effectively. It was enough to convince Florence that nurses needed professional training to teach them basic medical procedures and simple self-discipline.

Florence herself usually worked for 20 hours a day. She often tended to the wounded soldiers individually after 8:30 p.m., when the other nurses were banned from the wards. During this time, she talked to the wounded and helped them write letters home. The soldiers described Florence as a savior with a magic touch who always seemed to be on hand to help.

In 1855, the *Illustrated London News* published a sketch of Florence tending to patients while holding a lamp. The image made Florence instantly famous in England.

From that point on, Florence would always be remembered as the Lady with the Lamp—a guardian angel for the wounded and unwell.

By 1855, Florence had greatly improved conditions at the Scutari hospital, but her own health suffered as a result. In May, Florence collapsed from exhaustion.

It took 10 days for her to recover from a fever that the doctor described as one of the worst he had seen. But Florence would never fully recover. At the time, no one was sure what affected her, but today doctors think it was a disease called brucellosis. Brucellosis causes fever, shaking, aches, pains, depression, and exhaustion. These were all symptoms Florence suffered from for the rest of her life.

After the Crimean War ended and all of her patients had sailed home, Florence returned to England. She was now very famous. A biography on her had been published, thousands of people had written her fan mail, and porcelain figures had been made in her likeness. In response this, the British government planned a big celebration to welcome her home. But Florence didn't want a fuss made of her. She entered England under a fake name and surprised her family at Lea Hurst by walking across the fields unannounced to the house.

Florence would continue to shun the limelight for the rest of her life. But she also worked tirelessly until her death. She met the British queen, Queen Victoria, to tell her about the desperate changes needed in army hospitals. On Florence's recommendation, Queen Victoria ordered a Royal Commission be set up to reform army hospitals. The commission later implemented almost all of the improvements that Florence had suggested.

From 1857, Florence became too unwell to leave the house and instead worked from her couch. Soon after, she published *Notes on Nursing*. This textbook established rules for modern nursing and was used to train nurses for years to come. Informed by the horrific conditions and high death rates at Scutari Hospital, Florence now advocated hygiene as being an important factor in preventing the spread of disease.

Some of these nurses trained at the Nightingale School for Nurses at St. Thomas's Hospital in London. Florence was able to set up the school in 1860 with

£45,000 ($76,500) of donations made by her adoring public.

The Nightingale School was the first of its kind in the world. Its nurses were taught practical skills such as applying bandages and leeches and ensuring a high level of sanitation in the hospital wards. Florence's nurses were highly thought of and quickly obtained important jobs in hospitals across Great Britain. It is for this reason that Florence laid the foundations for modern nursing.

Florence died in 1910, after 50 years of being bound to her bed and sofa. However, she had done the unimaginable in her time. She resisted the expectations put upon her to marry and have children instead of work. Florence showed that women were capable of making a huge contribution to modern society.

Her achievements were highly celebrated. In 1907, she became the first woman to receive the Order of Merit, one of the greatest honors of the British Empire. But Florence made it clear she did not want a fuss after she died. Britain's King George V offered to have Florence buried at a special church in London called Westminster Abbey, which was another great honor. But instead, Florence's family buried her, as instructed, near her parents' home in Hampshire, England. A simple cross marking her grave reads "F. N. Born 1820. Died 1910."

Sarah G. Bagley:
Evils of Factory Life

Sarah G. Bagley was a labor activist who founded one of the first unions for women in the United States. Sarah is best known for leading the female workers of Lowell, Massachusetts, to protest against the conditions at the town's mills. Sarah was seen as a rabble-rouser by the mill companies and as a hero by her coworkers. But she was a reluctant hero.

At first, Sarah liked working in the mills. She even wrote a newspaper article praising the "Pleasures of Factory Life." But within a few years, her views had changed. She began writing about the miserable conditions in the factories and urged workers to fight for change. In doing so, Sarah paved the way for the rights of female workers in the United States.

Sarah George Bagley was born on April 19, 1806, in Candia, New Hampshire. Her parents were farmers who also owned a small mill. Like most Americans at the time, the family worked on the land rather than living in a city.

Back then, textile items such as thread and cloth were made in homes rather than in factories. However, this changed in the 1820s, as the United States moved into an industrial age and textile mills opened in the Northeast. The mills used the same large machines as those used in the United Kingdom at the time. They could produce far greater quantities of cloth than women could make in their homes. Soon, factory owners were advertising for young women to leave their farms and work in the new emerging mill towns.

One of these towns was Lowell, Massachusetts, which had been built entirely around its mill factories. The first factory opened in 1823, and by 1840 there were more than 30 factories in Lowell. Known as the City of Spindles, Lowell impressed many important visitors, such as English author Charles Dickens. Dickens found Lowell completely unlike an English factory town. It was new and clean, and the female workers who made up over two-thirds of the workforce seemed healthy, well dressed, and happy.

For Sarah, going to work in Lowell was appealing. Like many farmers' daughters, becoming a mill girl would allow Sarah to be independent from her family and earn some money. In turn, the mill companies cared for young female workers. They provided boardinghouses for them as well as a library and lectures, so the girls could expand their minds. This system was called Paternalism.

When Sarah moved to Lowell in 1836, the boardinghouse was her first shock. She had to share a bunkhouse with five other women and the lights were switched out at 10 p.m. But Sarah soon made friends with her roommates and enjoyed her surroundings. The mill where she worked paid $1.25 out of her weekly salary to the boardinghouse keeper, who did all of the cooking and cleaning. Suddenly, Sarah had gone from farmer's daughter to city worker and was surrounded by new friends. She even enjoyed her work at the Hamilton Manufacturing Company mill.

Like all new mill workers, Sarah started off as a spare hand or an apprentice to a senior worker, who showed her the ropes. At 31, Sarah was slightly older than many of the mill girls, who were usually between 15 and 30. She quickly became skilled at using the power looms. These were giant machines that made cloth from the threads created by the other machines in the mill.

By the end of her first year, Sarah was earning the top rate for a weaver—60 cents a day. Despite working a long, 73-hour week—the average for mill girls in the 1830s and 1840s—Sarah liked her factory work well enough to write an approving article on it. Sarah's "Pleasures of Factory Life" appeared in the *Lowell Offering*, a mill newspaper written by its workers:

> Pleasures there are, even in factory life; and we have many... Who can closely examine all the movements of the complicated, curious machinery, and not be led to the reflection, that the mind is boundless, and is destined to rise higher and still higher; and that it can accomplish almost any thing on which it fixes its attention!... In Lowell, we enjoy abundant means of information, especially in the way of public lectures... Most of us, when at home, live in the country, and therefore cannot enjoy these privileges.

Not all of the women working in the Lowell mills shared Sarah's view of a pleasurable factory life. In 1834 and 1836, female mill workers went on strike over a proposed pay cut. Neither of these strikes ended well. The strikers were fired and a pay cut was introduced. But it was the first sign that Lowell mill girls were willing to speak out against the conditions imposed by their employers.

When Sarah joined the Lowell workforce in 1836, there was little talk of another strike. In that year, a financial crisis set off an economic recession that lasted until 1843. During this time, profits and wages throughout the United States went down and unemployment went up. The Lowell mills twice cut the pay of their female workers, saying it was either that or the mills would have to close.

Some of the mill girls had to be laid off anyway, and those still employed in Lowell did not dare protest against the pay cuts. But after the recession passed, wages stayed down and conditions in the mill factories worsened. Soon there would be a new labor movement in Lowell, and it would be led by Sarah G. Bagley.

To start with, however, Sarah tried to keep her head down and avoid trouble. In the early 1840s, the mills in Lowell announced speed ups for their weavers. This meant that a weaver had to use two looms at once, instead of one. To prevent the strain of this extra work, Sarah changed jobs and became a dresser. This involved applying starch to thread that was then used in the power looms. But the weavers at the nearby Middlesex

Manufacturing Company protested against the speed ups by going on strike. The strike ended in a devastating defeat, with those who protested being fired and blacklisted from working in any Lowell mill again. The treatment of the strikers deeply affected Sarah. But despite her feelings, Sarah went to work as a weaver for the Middlesex Manufacturing Company, which now had vacancies to fill.

Sarah now saw factory life differently. Two decades after the factories had opened in Lowell, conditions for workers had become increasingly poor. The factories were stiflingly hot and poorly ventilated. The machines were deafeningly loud and often caused serious accidents. A new lighting system enabled workers to keep toiling away after dark, increasing their average workday to 14 hours.

In addition, the workers lived their lives according to a series of bells. These signaled the start of the day at 5 a.m., a half-hour lunch break at 12:30 p.m., and the day's end at 7:30 p.m.

Suddenly, the life that had promised Sarah freedom and financial independence felt more like a prison. But any mill girls who protested would be fired, evicted from their boardinghouses, and blacklisted from working in a Lowell mill again.

Sarah tried to voice her concerns by writing articles about the worsening conditions for the *Lowell Offering*. But the paper rejected her articles, instead preferring to print positive mill stories like "Pleasures of Factory Life."

In 1844, Sarah had had enough and decided to take action. In Lowell, the working men had a union called the New England

Workingman's Association (NEWA). The NEWA even had its own newspaper, the *Voice of Industry*. Sarah said that there should also be a union that represented the working women of Lowell. With this in mind, she formed the Lowell Female Labor Reform Association (LFLRA). It was one of the first labor organizations for women in the United States.

The first meeting of the LFLRA was held one snowy December night in a local hall. Of the 20 women who had braved the weather, all were appointed officers of the LFLRA, and Sarah became the president. Together, the mill girls came up with a motto for the LFLRA—"Try again." They said this would help them remember to never give up the fight.

Sarah's first plan was to shorten the mill girls' working hours. But instead of striking, Sarah wanted the government to make a 10-hour workday the law. To do this, she collected the signatures of over 2,000 Lowell mill girls in a petition to the Massachusetts legislature. This petitioning became known as the Ten Hour Day Movement.

We the undersigned peaceable, industrious and hardworking men and women of Lowell, in view of our condition—the evils already come upon us, by toiling from 13 to 14 hours per day, confined in unhealthy apartments, exposed to the poisonous contagion of air, vegetable, animal and mineral properties, debarred from proper Physical Exercise, Mental discipline, and Mastication cruelly limited, and thereby hastening us on through pain, disease and privation, down to a premature grave, pray the legislature to institute a ten-hour working day in all of the factories of the state.

—Signed Sarah G. Bagley and 2,000 others, January 15, 1845

In response to the petition, the Massachusetts legislature ordered a committee to investigate the conditions at the Lowell mills. The fact that its petition had led to such an action was a major victory for the LFLRA. Sarah was one of nine mill workers ordered to testify before the committee. She told them:

> The chief evil, so far as health is concerned, is the shortness of time allowed for meals. The next evil the length of time employed— not giving them [the mill girls] time to cultivate their minds.

The committee also talked to the owner of Boott Cotton Mill, whose evidence was vastly different from Sarah's. He said the mill workers "were not driven by wretchedness and hunger" and had families they could return to at any time.

When the committee issued its report, the news was not good for the LFLRA. The report said that working in the mill was no worse for people's health than any other indoor job and that changes to the law were not required. It said working hours at the mills were a matter for the owners and their employees to discuss.

This was a bitter blow for the LFLRA. Sarah wrote a stinging attack on the committee in the *Voice of Industry*. Her article said many of the facts had been left out of the report and the mill girls' testimony had been twisted around.

The LFLRA, however, decided to stick to its "Try again" motto and submitted another petition in 1846. This one contained over 4,000 signatures from the mill workers of Lowell. But again, the committee refused to take action.

By 1846, Sarah G. Bagley had become a well-known labor figure. She quit working at the mill and traveled around New England to union conventions. There, she spoke about the rights of female workers and recruited members to the LFLRA.

Sarah became increasingly angry about a society in which men held all the important jobs and women were only thought fit for menial labor. She said the mills in Lowell were an example of that. The Paternalism system meant that mill owners were supposed to take care of their female workers, but instead they controlled and exploited them.

Sarah wrote about her views in the *Voice of Industry*, which she became editor of that year. Sarah introduced a female department to the newspaper, to discuss issues concerning women. To show how far she had come since her "Pleasures of Factory Life" article, Sarah now published articles with titles such as "Evils of Factory Life." Some of these articles were so strong they could not be published in the *Voice*, but instead appeared in pamphlets called *Factory Tracts*.

Then, in June 1846, everything changed. Sarah had a disagreement with the new editor of the *Voice*, who said he did not want a female department at the newspaper. This upset Sarah enough to also resign as president of the LFLRA.

Sarah was tired of fighting and decided to take a new job as the first female telegraph operator in the United States. She helped people write their messages and tapped them out from the telegraph office in Lowell.

But, despite paving the way for women in the job, Sarah was dismayed to find out she was being paid less than the man she had replaced. She wrote to a friend, Mrs. Martin, about the continuing need for women to fight for equality.

Sarah wrote that she was:

sick at heart when I look into the social world and see woman so willingly made a dupe to the beastly selfishness of man.

Over the next few years, Sarah traveled around New England writing about prison reform, health care, and women's rights. However, little is known about her life after she left Lowell, and it is unclear when she died.

Although the LFLRA disbanded in 1848, other labor activists kept fighting for a shorter workday in Lowell. Finally, in 1874, the Massachusetts legislature made a 10-hour workday for all workers the law. It was what Sarah G. Bagley and the mill girls had been fighting for.

For this reason, Sarah is considered a labor pioneer. She led the way for American female workers to stand up for their rights in a workforce they had only just joined. This enabled others after Sarah to pick up where she left off and continue the fight for equal rights for women workers.

Mother Jones:
The Most Dangerous Woman in America

Mother Jones was the leading American female labor activist of the late 19th and early 20th century.

She spent her life traveling around the country organizing strikes and urging coal miners and mill workers to stand up for their rights. Mother Jones was a fiery and determined activist who would never give up the fight. But to the outside world, she looked like a harmless old woman. Dressed in black and wearing glasses, Mother Jones was able to cross picket lines and walk into mills without arousing suspicion. For this skill, Mother

Jones was once called "the most dangerous woman in America."

Mary Harris was born in Cork, Ireland, in 1837. It was a difficult time for the country. When she was eight years old, a disease caused Ireland's potato crop to fail. Potatoes were the main source of food for many people in Ireland, and without them a widespread famine struck. Hundreds of thousands of people left Ireland as a result, Mary's family among them. Her family moved to Canada and then settled in the United States.

When Mary grew up, she studied to be a teacher and married an iron worker named George Jones. Like many workers during the Industrial Revolution, George worked in a factory. He also belonged to a union, which stood up for the conditions and treatment of its members. The Jones family lived in a small room in Memphis, Tennessee. It was there that Mary gave birth to four children.

But in 1867, disaster struck the Jones family. Mary's husband, George, caught a deadly yellow fever sweeping through Memphis and died. Then, one after another, Mary's children also died from the disease. Because only medical people with permits were allowed to enter Mary's diseased neighborhood, she had to cope with her grief alone. All day and night, Mary could hear the wheels of the death cart outside, picking up the bodies of the dead. She decided to pack up her life and move to Chicago to start again.

In Chicago, Mary started a dressmaking business with a friend. The city of Chicago was growing quickly at that time. The city's railroads, rivers, and canals meant that goods could easily be transported in and out of its factories. But there was also a growing divide between the city's rich and its poor.

In her autobiography, Mary wrote about seeing the plight of Chicago's poor from the houses of her rich customers.

> I would look out of the plate glass windows and see the poor, shivering wretches, jobless and hungry walking along the frozen lake. The contrast of their conditions with that of the tropical comfort of the people for whom I sewed was painful to me. My employers seemed neither to notice nor to care.

In 1871, disaster struck once again. A great fire swept through Chicago, destroying many of the buildings. Mary's dressmaker's shop was burned to the ground. With all of her belongings lost, Mary decided to once again start over. This time, she would devote herself to helping American workers, many of whom were struggling to survive.

By the 1880s, the Industrial Revolution was in full swing in the United States. Steam now powered the machines that used to be powered by rivers. This meant that factories could be built anywhere. Coal was mined in great quantities and burned to create steam for the factory machines. Many workers had arrived from European countries such as Ireland and would work for cheap wages. Because of this, owners of mills, factories, and coal mines could afford to pay their workers very little. In reaction to these low wages and poor conditions, many workers went on strike.

In 1877, a railroad strike in Chicago spread and became a nationwide strike of over 100,000 workers across the country. But there was no one in charge to help the workers fight for better conditions, and they went back to work.

Mary decided she would help organize worker strikes and protests. In the 1890s, she became an organizer for the United Mine Workers (UMW). It would be the start of her new life as a labor activist. From that point on, she would live "with no abiding place, but wherever a fight is on against wrong."

Mary traveled to coal-mining towns to set up branches of the UMW and encourage badly treated miners to strike. Although Mary was only 43 in 1890, she looked much older in her long black dresses and glasses. This often helped her sneak into places she wasn't allowed go, such as factories, coal mines, and behind picket lines. Despite looking like a harmless old woman, Mary gained a fierce reputation as a fighter for the workers. They even gave her a nickname—Mother Jones.

In 1891, the UMW sent Mother Jones to Arnot, Pennsylvania, to convince miners there to stay out on strike. The miners had been striking for nearly a month and were hungry, tired, and running out of steam. To make matters worse, the mine company had brought in strikebreakers, also known as scab workers, to replace the miners.

When Mother Jones arrived, she had a meeting with the miners and then went to her room in the local hotel. But the hotel was owned by the mine, and she was turned away.

Mother Jones stayed the night with a local miner, but when the mine owner found out, he evicted the miner and his family. Mother Jones said the sight of the miner's family being thrown out of their home, with their possessions piled up on a cart, gave the strikers a new burst of energy.

However, the next day, Mother Jones told the miners to stay at home and not picket the mines as usual. Instead, she asked the miners' wives to arm themselves with mops and brooms. In the morning, these miners' wives stood outside the mine and stopped the scabs from entering by hitting them with their brooms.

In her autobiography, Mother Jones said the miners' wives kept a constant guard.

*Every day women with brooms or mops
in one hand and babies in the other arm
wrapped in little blankets went to the mines
and watched that no one went in. And all
night long they kept watch. They were
heroic women.*

After several years, the Arnot mine owners finally gave in and agreed to some of the miners' demands. It was a famous victory for Mother Jones.

Next, Mother Jones turned her attentions to helping child workers. According to the 1900 census, one out of every six American children under 16 worked full time. Of these children, boys most commonly worked in coal mines, and girls worked in mill factories. In states such as Massachusetts and Pennsylvania, mill towns hired the daughters of coal miners or farmers. Sarah G. Bagley, a farmer's daughter, had been hired to work at a mill.

Mother Jones had been told that these children suffered under terrible working conditions. To find out for herself, Mother Jones visited the coal mines to observe the working conditions for the boys. Here, breaker boys between 10 and 14 years old worked for 10 hours a day, six days a week, sorting pieces of coal that rushed down a conveyor belt. Mother Jones reported that these breaker boys had deformed backs and fingers from their work, which paid around 60 cents a day.

Mother Jones then went to observe conditions in the mills of the South. Here, she described seeing seven-year-old girls working from 5:30 a.m. until 7 p.m. for only $2 or $3 a week.

Mother Jones wrote:

I have watched them all day long tending the dangerous machinery. I have seen their helpless limbs torn off.

In 1903, the workers from 600 mills in Philadelphia had had enough of their working conditions and went on strike. The mill workers wanted a reduction in their work week, from 60 to 55 hours.

But neither the mill owners, the state legislature, nor the newspapers were interested in the mill workers' demands. One reporter told Mother Jones that the newspapers wouldn't cover the strike because they were partly owned by the mill companies.

Determined to bring the plight of the children to the public's attention, Mother

Jones organized a march of the mill children, often called the Children's Crusade. This led the mill strikers, including 100 boys and girls, on a march from Philadelphia to New York City. The journey lasted for three weeks, and the children carried signs with statements such as "We want to go to school" and "55 hours or nothing."

The marchers stayed with union families and sympathetic hotels and were often fed by local farmers. In the towns they passed through, Mother Jones gave speeches, which were reported in the local and national newspapers. She announced the marchers would not stop until they reached the president's home in Oyster Bay, New York. Here, they would ask President Theodore Roosevelt to pass a law protecting child workers.

But when the marchers reached Oyster Bay, they were told the president was not there. The president's secretary instead told Mother Jones to write a letter to President Roosevelt. It was a big disappointment for the marchers, but Mother Jones did write a letter. In it, she pleaded with the president to aid the plight of child workers, who she had seen "with hands, fingers and other parts of their little bodies mutilated because of their childish ignorance of machinery."

President Roosevelt said he was sympathetic, but it was up to each state to pass its own laws. The marchers had no choice except to go home and back to work.

The Children's Crusade had done a lot to raise public awareness of child labor. It also turned Mother Jones into a well-known labor activist. Yet the United States did not pass a national law restricting child labor until 1938.

In 1912, Mother Jones was sent to a strike being held by miners of Paint and Cabin Creeks in West Virginia. Things there had turned nasty when the mine companies brought in strikebreakers and evicted families from their company-owned houses.

Many of these families and their possessions were put on trains by armed mine company guards and dumped along the tracks. The families then had no choice but to camp outside in groups that became known as tent colonies. Soon these colonies began to suffer from hunger and diseases caused by unsanitary conditions. Mother Jones helped the best she could.

Meanwhile, the mine companies ordered their guards to protect the mines against the strikers.

Mother Jones urged the West Virginia miners not to give in to the mining companies by returning to work. But the company guards were making life difficult for the strikers by blocking the roads that were owned by the mines.

Once, after giving a speech, guards armed with machine guns stopped Mother Jones as she traveled down the road. According to her autobiography, Mother Jones put her hand over the gun's barrel and told them to let her through. They did.

But the situation in West Virginia soon spiraled out of control. A gun battle broke out between the strikers and mine company guards, and a miner was killed. In response, the governor of West Virginia ordered a period of martial law. This meant the army would take control of the area. Dozens of strikers and union officials were arrested by the army, including Mother Jones. No company guards were arrested.

Mother Jones had been arrested before in West Virginia, in 1902, and had stood trial there. The prosecuting lawyer had even called her "the most dangerous woman in America" for helping the striking coal miners. But now, Mother Jones was charged with "conspiracy that resulted in murder." A guilty verdict would mean the death sentence.

Mother Jones was kept in jail for three months awaiting her trial. She had to fight off rats in her cell with an empty bottle. But she stayed strong while in prison. She said:

> I am 80 years old and I haven't long to live anyhow. Since I have to die, I would rather die for the cause to which I have given so much of my life.

Eventually, things ended well for Mother Jones. The U.S. Senate investigated the governor's decision to enact martial law, and Mother Jones was quickly released from jail. The mine companies were made to recognize the miners' union and give in to some of its demands. It was a major victory for the UMW and Mother Jones.

Her time in prison had created a lot of publicity, and articles in the newspapers had made the public aware of the miners' struggle. Many members of the public and politicians became sympathetic toward the miners. Over time, conditions improved for many.

After the West Virginia strikes, Mother Jones kept traveling around the United States to give speeches and help striking workers. In the 1920s, she published her autobiography.

When she died in 1930, Mother Jones was buried in a coal-mining cemetery in Illinois. Because she had fought alongside the miners and mill workers, she was considered one of them. Mother Jones is today remembered as a labor activist who never gave up the fight for fair pay and conditions for ordinary workers.

> All the average human being asks is something he can call home; a family that is fed and warm; and now and then a little happiness.
>
> —Mother Jones

Continuing the Fight

During the Industrial Revolutions of the United States and the United Kingdom, upper- and middle-class women were expected to marry, stay at home, and raise their children. Working-class women were expected to work in menial jobs for less money than men.

Elizabeth, Florence, Sarah, and Mother Jones broke out of these traditional roles. They brought about major reforms in prisons, health care, and workers' rights. They also showed that women are as capable as men. Their work paved the way for women to demand the same opportunities and rights as men.

Other Important Figures

Annie Besant (1847–1933)

Annie Besant was a British social reformer who campaigned for the rights of the match girls. These were female workers of the Bryant and May match factory, who worked for 14 hours a day and were fined for talking or dropping matches. The matches also contained yellow phosphorus, which caused hair loss and "phossy jaw," a fatal form of cancer. Annie shamed the company in a newspaper article and formed a union of the match girls. After a strike, Bryant and May changed its working conditions and eventually stopped using yellow phosphorus in its matches.

Agnes Nestor (1880–1948)

Agnes Nestor was an American labor leader who helped form the International Glove Workers Union. Agnes led a strike against her glove factory employers, who charged their workers for needles, machine oil, and machine rental. After 10 days of the strike, the glove company agreed to the strikers' demands. Agnes later held positions in the Chicago and national Women's Trade Union League. Agnes is remembered as a skilled union negotiator who fought for a minimum wage for workers and against child labor.

Jane Addams (1860–1935)

Jane Addams was an American social reformer and cowinner of the Nobel Prize for Peace in 1931. Jane is best known for setting up Hull House in Chicago in 1889. Hull House was a settlement house that offered services such as classes, daycare, and a library for poorer people in the area. Jane also worked with several labor, reform, and social work groups and helped found the American Civil Liberties Union (ACLU) in 1920.

Timeline

1795   Riots break out in several English towns over the rising cost of bread. The high cost has been caused by a poor wheat harvest in 1794.

1814   Businessman Francis Cabot Lowell builds the first industrial spinning and weaving machines in the United States, based on models he has seen in the United Kingdom.

1823   The Gaols Act makes it law in the United Kingdom for prison guards to be paid a salary and for female guards to watch female inmates. The use of iron restraints is prohibited.

1836   Theodor Fliedner opens the German Kaiserswerth Institute. It has been partly inspired by Elizabeth Fry's prison reform work in London.

1840 Elizabeth Fry's training school for nurses is set up at Guy's Hospital in London. It has been partly modeled on the German Kaiserswerth Institute.

1844 The Lowell Female Labor Reform Association (LFLRA) is founded by Sarah G. Bagley.

1845 The potato famine in Ireland begins. Hundreds of thousands of Irish immigrants move to the United States to find work in the 1840s.

1853 Mill owners in Lowell, Massachusetts, agree to shorten their employees' workday to 11 hours.

1854 The United Kingdom and France send troops to help Turkey fight Russia in the Crimean War.

1857 A Royal Commission on the Health of the Army is established, based on Florence Nightingale's recommendation to Queen Victoria.

1860 The Nightingale School for Nurses opens at St. Thomas's Hospital in London.

1867 A yellow fever epidemic sweeps through Memphis, Tennessee, killing over 500 people. It is one of several epidemics to strike Memphis between 1828 and 1879.

1868 The last British convicts bound for Australia under the transportation system land in New South Wales.

1871 The Great Chicago Fire kills 300 people and leaves over 100,000 people homeless.

1877 The Great Railroad Strike starts in West Virginia and soon spreads nationwide. It lasts for 45 days and involves over 100,000 strikers.

1890 The United Mine Workers (UMW) union is formed as a result of a merger between the Knights of Labor and the National Progressive Miners Union.

1902 The last execution at Newgate Prison takes place before the prison is demolished later that year.

1924 The city of Lowell, Massachusetts, reaches its peak as a textile manufacturing center.

1938 The United States passes the Fair Labor Standards Act. It prohibits anyone under age 14 from working during school hours.

Find Out More

Books

McDaniel, Melissa. *The Industrial Revolution* (Cornerstones of Freedom). New York: Children's Press, 2012.

Morris, Neil. *The Industrial Revolution* (Research It!). Chicago: Heinemann Library, 2010.

Staton, Hilarie N. *The Industrial Revolution* (All About America). New York: Kingfisher, 2012.

Web sites

Facthound offers a safe, fun way to find Internet sites related to this book. All of the sites on Facthound have been researched by our staff.

Here's all you do:

Visit www.facthound.com

Type in this code: 9781484608630

Glossary

activist person who takes action to bring about social or political change

anesthetic type of medicine that reduces feelings of pain

boardinghouse private house that people pay to stay and have meals in

committee group of people put together to investigate or report on something

convict person serving a sentence after being found guilty of a crime

flogging beaten with a stick or whip as a punishment

leech bloodsucking worm often used by doctors in the 19th century to bleed people

martial law period when the government is ruled by the military, which often occurs at times of dangerous and violent unrest

picket stand outside a workplace in protest during a strike and persuade others not to enter

plight difficult, dangerous, or desperate situation for a person or group

Quaker member of a Christian group also known as the Society of Friends, which supports peace and is against war

rabble-rouser someone who stirs up strong emotions in groups of others

recession period of economic decline with reduced industrial activity

sanitation process of keeping a place clean of disease, often by providing clean water and disposing of sewage

slum dirty and overcrowded part of a city, inhabited by people living in poverty

textile cloth or woven fabric

union organization of workers who protect the interests of their members

Index